What's Hatching Out of That Egg?

What's Hatching Out of That Egg?

by Patricia Lauber

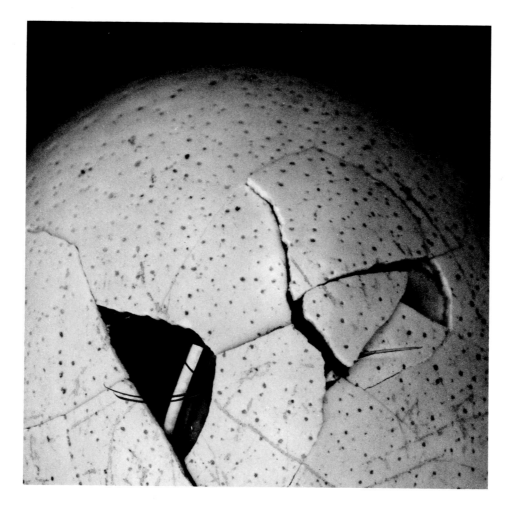

Crown Publishers, Inc.
New York

Text copyright © 1979 by Patricia Lauber

Published by Crown Publishers, Inc., 225 Park Avenue South, New York, New York 10003 and represented in Canada by the Canadian MANDA Group

CROWN is a trademark of Crown Publishers, Inc.

Manufactured in the United States of America

Library of Congress Cataloging-in-Publication Data
Lauber, Patricia. What's hatching out of that egg? Summary: Text and illustrations introduce a variety of eggs and the animals that hatch out of them. Includes ostrich, python, bullfrog, and monarch butterfly eggs among others. 1. Animals—Infancies of—Juvenile literature. 2. Reproduction—Juvenile literature. [1. Animals—Infancy. 2. Reproduction] I. Title. QL763.L38   C1979
591.3'9   79-12054

ISBN 0-517-53724-9
0-517-56349-5 (pbk.)

10 9 8 7 6 5 4

What's Hatching Out of That Egg?

Eggs All Over

Eggs are everywhere. They're in seas, lakes, streams, ponds, and puddles. They're in tree stumps and in the ground. They're glued to the undersides of leaves. They're even tucked away around your home—in closets, corners, flower pots.

You are about to meet some of these eggs. Try to guess what kind they are. Study the photographs for clues. Study the text for more clues. Keep guessing until you discover what animal is hatching out of each egg.

Remember, some young animals look like their parents. Others don't at first. They may not even look like the same kind of animal.

Now turn the page and begin. Good luck!

Des Bartlett/Bruce Coleman

This egg is shiny, white, and big. It is even bigger than you see here. The mother laid it in a nest the father dug. She laid some twelve eggs in all.

Every day for seven weeks the mother sat on the nest. She rested her head and long neck on the ground. Her body looked like a big rock. At night the father sat on the nest. When hatching time came near, the young animals started to peep inside the eggs, and the parents peeped back. The young learned to know their parents' voices.

Now the first egg is hatching. The baby animal has grown so big that the shell is tight. The baby gives a strong push with its neck. The shell cracks, and a piece pops out. The baby lies back, rests, and looks out this window.

When it has rested, the baby pushes with its neck and legs. Suddenly the shell breaks open, and pieces fly into the air. The baby stretches and peeps.

Des Bartlett/Bruce Coleman

Clem Haagner/Bruce Coleman

Out at last! Now you can see that the baby is a bird—and it's a tired one. Hatching out of an egg is hard work. The baby rests in the nest for a day or so. Around it other chicks are hatching out, too. Soon they are all up and about. They are big babies. Each one stands about a foot high. They grow fast. As adults, they will be big birds. You may have seen some of these birds in a zoo.

The parents stay with their young and guard them. Those are the father's feet and legs you see. The father has very long legs and is a fast runner. He stands six or seven feet tall and weighs more than two hundred pounds. He is a bird that cannot fly.

These birds are . . .

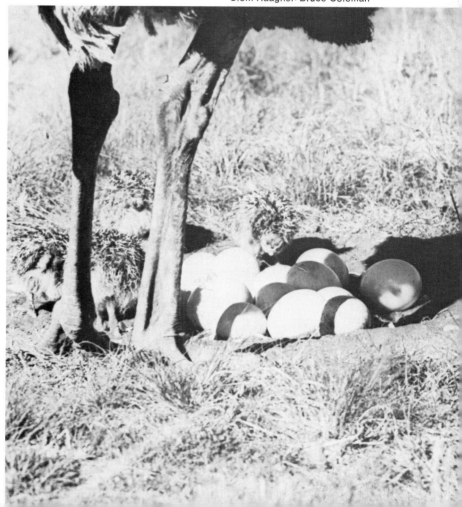

11

ostriches. They are the biggest birds alive, and they lay the biggest eggs. The father has shiny black feathers with white tips on his wings and tail. The mother has brown feathers.

Most wild ostriches live in Africa. A male ostrich may take one mate or three or four. The oldest female ostrich is the top hen. She lays the most eggs, and she sits on the nest.

Ostriches often join herds of zebras, antelope, and other animals that eat plants. As these animals feed, they stir up insects. The ostriches eat the insects, as well as lizards, fruits, flowers, or seeds that they may find. Because of their long necks, ostriches can see enemies far away. If the ostriches start to run, the zebras and antelope run too.

Leonard Lee Rue III

Thie big nest is in a swamp in the South. The mother animal built it. She bit off some plants. She took others in her jaws and tore them out by their roots. Still others she cut down with her tail. She piled the plants into this big mound.

The nest is near water. That's where this mother lives and finds her food. She leaves the water mostly to sun herself and also to lay her eggs.

The nest has a hollow at its top. The mother laid about thirty eggs there and then covered them and crawled away. But don't go near the nest. The mother is close by. You'd be sorry if she caught you!

The summer sun warms the eggs. So does the nest. As the plants rot, they give off heat. Two months go by. The baby animals are growing too big for their shells. The shells swell, then crack, but still the young are not out. Inside each shell is a thin, tough skin, which a baby must tear open before it can hatch.

Each baby has a hard knob at the end of its nose. It presses against the skin with the knob. The skin tears open. The knob is called an egg tooth. It drops off soon after a baby hatches. This baby is sticking its nose out for the first time.

Ross E. Hutchins

Here comes one baby animal. Others are hatching out around it. The newly hatched babies start to grunt. The mother hears them and comes to the nest. She opens the top. Then the babies head for the water all by themselves. They are able to crawl and swim.

The baby looks like its mother, but it is much smaller. It hunts the way she does. It catches its food with its front teeth and crushes the food with its back teeth. Then it swallows the food. The baby eats tiny fish and tadpoles and water beetles. It also eats bits of food that fall out of its mother's mouth.

The young are good hunters. But they, too, are hunted and eaten. Many are eaten by big fish, snakes, wading birds, and bobcats. Once they grow up, other animals leave them alone. You'll see why when you turn the page.

These animals are . . .

Ross E. Hutchins

Florida News Bureau

alligators. A big male may be fifteen feet long and weigh six hundred pounds. He has strong jaws and lots of sharp teeth.

A mother alligator may stay with her young for several months. When spring comes, she leaves. It is time for her to mate, to build a nest, and to lay more eggs.

In late summer, the mother finds a good place to leave her eggs. It may be tree bark or a twig or the underside of a leaf or stone. She spins a pad of silk and lays her eggs on it. Then she spins a silk covering for the eggs. This is an egg sac. The spinning takes several hours. The finished egg sac is about an inch long. It is tough and brown. It looks like this.

The mother has many relatives. Some kinds guard their eggs. Some kinds carry their egg sacs around with them. Some even carry their young on their backs. This mother does not stay with her eggs. When cold weather comes, she dies.

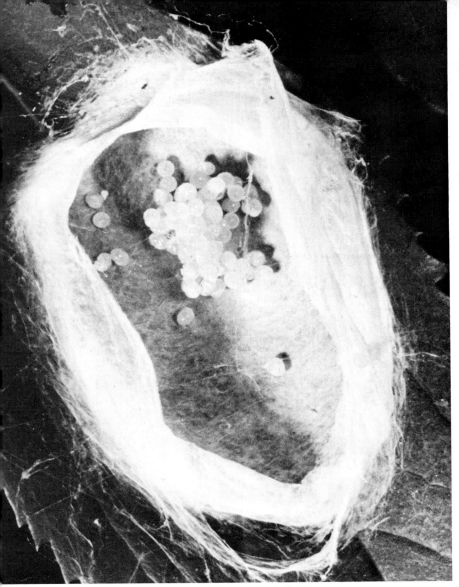

This egg sac has been cut open to show what's inside. A sac usually holds at least one hundred eggs. It may hold as many as six hundred.

The young hatch out of their eggs inside the sac. Each one cuts its way out of the egg, using its sharp egg tooth. After they have hatched, the young stay in the sac, and they grow. These animals have no bones. Instead, each has a hard covering on its body. From time to time the covering is shed. Then the animal grows some more.

When the weather warms up, the young tear open the egg sac. They swarm out. Some people think these animals are insects, but they are not. Insects have six legs, and these young animals have eight. They also have eight eyes, but they don't see well.

How are they all going to find places to live? They're going to fly away on the wind.

A young animal climbs up on something and stands facing the wind. Threads of silk are spun out of its body, and these act as a parachute. When the wind catches the parachute, the young animal is carried away. Some may land on ships at sea or on airplanes. Most are carried miles away to new homes.

These animals live in gardens, fields, and parks. They trap insects for food. They are . . .

spiders, garden spiders. Their traps are the webs they spin. Some spiders sit in the middle of the web and wait for an insect to be trapped. Other kinds of spiders wait at the side of the web.

Watch for spiders at work. See how the web is made. See how food is trapped. Be patient. A spider's work takes time.

Spring is the time to look for these eggs. A pond is a good place to find them. Look among the water plants growing near the edge.

The father moved into this pond in early spring. Every evening he called for a mate. Perhaps you heard him. As darkness fell, his calls grew louder. The female he attracted laid these eggs. Each is tiny, round, and dark, and it is covered with a clear jelly. The eggs stick together in clumps.

Once the eggs are laid, the parents leave.

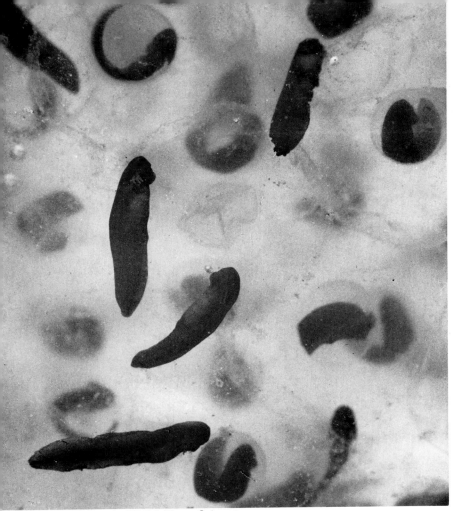

Inside the egg jelly, young animals have taken shape. Some are still inside the jelly, some are hatching out, and some are all the way out.

A newly hatched baby is tiny and helpless. It has no eyes or mouth. All it can do is stick to something, such as a water plant or the egg jelly. In a few days its eyes and mouth form. Its tail grows. Then it swims about and spends much of its time eating. It nibbles on water plants. It sucks out the soft parts of dead tadpoles, fishes, and insects. It is also likely to get eaten itself —by a fish, bird, frog, or snake.

The young animal looks like a fish, but it isn't. Its parents were not fish. So far, this young animal does not look like its parents, but it will soon. A big change is about to take place.

Now the young animal has grown legs. Many other changes are taking place in its body. During this time, the young animal does not eat. It lives on food stored in its tail. As the food is used up, the tail becomes smaller and smaller. One day it disappears. The young animal now looks like its parents. It lives the way they do: it breathes air, and it eats insects, which it catches on its long sticky tongue.

It is a . . .

frog. This one is a bullfrog. It is the biggest North American frog, and the best jumper.

All frogs lay eggs that hatch into tadpoles. Most tadpoles change into frogs in about two months. But the bullfrog tadpole takes longer. It stays a tadpole for one, two, or even three years.

Whose mother can this be? She lives in the sea, but she's not a fish. She has no backbone. Her body is soft, rubbery, and shaped like a bag. She's often hard to see. She can change color to match rocks, weeds, or sand.

This mother lives alone in dark places—in caves or old shipwrecks, under rocks, and in cracks. She eats lobsters, crabs, clams, oysters, and mussels. She may hunt for food, or she may wait for her meal to pass by. Then she reaches out a long arm and pulls it in.

After she mates, the mother goes back to living alone. She lays eggs that are shaped like tiny grains of rice. The eggs have stems that the mother weaves and glues together, making strings of eggs. She hangs the strings under a ledge or in a cave.

This mother stays with her eggs. She keeps them safe from hungry crabs and fishes. She blows water on them and runs her arms through the strings. That is how she keeps the eggs clean and changes the water around them.

The mother lays some 150,000 eggs, which hatch in about six weeks. During this time, the mother guards them. She does not eat. She only takes care of her eggs. When the young hatch, the mother's job is done. She dies about two weeks later. The young are on their own.

The newly hatched young are tiny. At first they do not look like their parents, but soon they will. Each one will grow eight arms. It will jet through the water; it will catch its own food. If it is in danger, it will shoot out an inky black cloud.

Each of these babies is an . . .

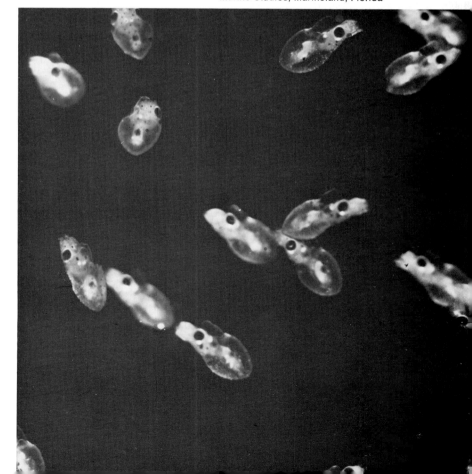

Robert C. Hermes/Photo Researchers, Inc.

octopus. This one is the common octopus. Other kinds of octopuses have eggs that look like bunches of grapes.

The common octopus is one of the best mothers in the sea. Few sea creatures take care of their eggs. The mother octopus takes good care of hers.

In the spring thousands of these animals pop out of the water every day. They head for their nesting places, which are called rookeries. Soon each rookery is crowded with 50,000 to 100,000 animals. The time has come to mate and to lay eggs. The animals gather stones to make their nests. Their home is a land where trees, bushes, and grasses cannot grow.

Courtship, nest building, and egg laying take about a month. During this time the animals never leave the rookery. They do not go to sea and feed. They live on their body fat.

Robert W. Hernandez/Photo Researchers, Inc.

A mother lays two eggs in her stony nest. Then she waddles off to feed at sea. The father keeps the eggs warm until the mother comes back two weeks later. Then it is his turn to feed, while the mother takes over the nest.

The young hatch out of the eggs in about a month. Here's one peeking out. It's a chick that is covered with the soft feathers called down. It does not look much like its parents.

The chicks are always hungry. The parents take turns sitting on the nest and going for food. The chicks cannot go to sea and feed themselves because their baby down is not waterproof.

The parents are kept busy feeding their young. The chicks eat and eat and grow quickly. They must. Summer is short here, and the chicks must be ready to swim away before winter comes.

U.S. Navy photo

Michael C. T. Smith/Photo Researchers, Inc.

The chicks have grown too big for their nests. Now both parents work full time to feed their young. Groups of big chicks huddle together while their parents are away. A few adults look after them.

Soon the chicks will lose their down and grow black and white feathers. They will be ready to feed themselves. They will be ready to spend the winter at sea, to swim north to the packs of ice. They will be gone before winter reaches Antarctica.

These birds are . . .

penguins. They are the kind called Adélie penguins. Here is a parent with a big chick trying to cram itself into the nest.

Penguins are birds that cannot fly. On land they waddle along, holding their flippers out for balance. They also slide on their bellies. But penguins are most at home in the sea. They swim as well as any fish.

Michael C. T. Smith/Photo Researchers, Inc.

Michael C. T. Smith/Photo Researchers, Inc.

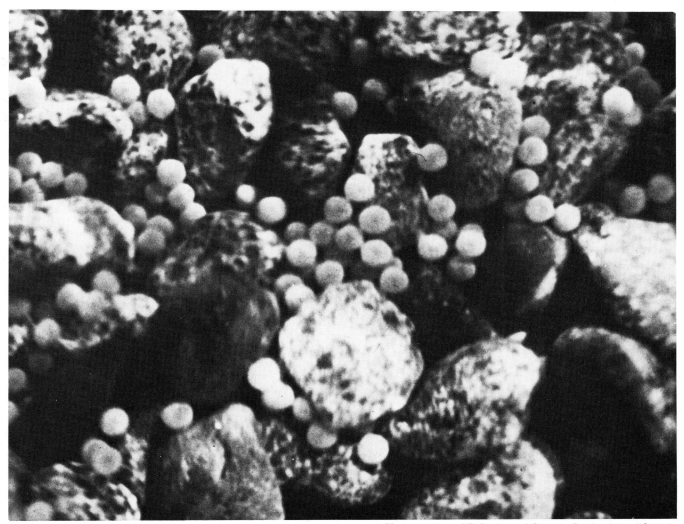

These small eggs are in a riverbed where the water is clean, shallow, and fast-running. The eggs are resting in a nest of gravel. The mother dug the nest while the father stood guard. It took her hours to dig a nest six inches deep. Now the parents are gone. The young will hatch out by themselves.

Here's one hatching out. What can it be?

Now you can see what the tiny animal looks like. Behind its tail you can see the eye of another young animal that will soon hatch out.

At first the young are helpless. They are not fully formed. For example, they do not have mouths yet, and they cannot catch food. How can they live without catching food?

Each tiny animal has its own food—the egg yolk. The yolk sac is what makes the big bulge. You can see blood vessels in the sac. They carry nourishment to the tiny animal, which grows and changes.

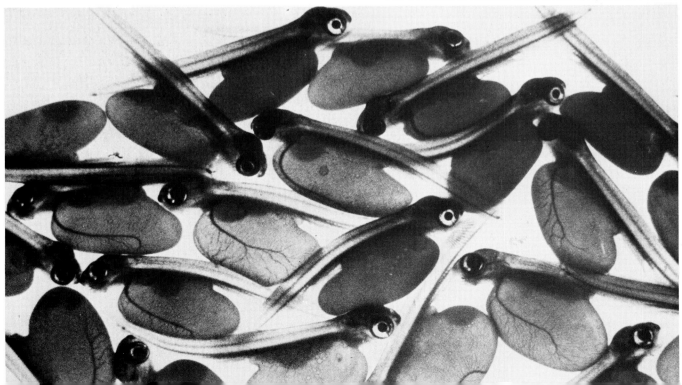

Now the yolk is nearly used up. The young animal has grown a lot, and it is beginning to look like its parents. By the time the yolk is gone, the young animal will be fully formed. It will be able to catch food in the water, and it will look like the sort of animal it really is. Do you know what that is?

This animal is a . . .

35

fish. What kind is it? Here are some clues. A few kinds of this fish spend their lives in fresh water. All the other kinds follow rivers to the sea. They live in the sea until they are ready to lay their eggs—to spawn. Then they go back to fresh water. Many find their way to the river where they were born.

Getting there isn't easy. Some must swim upstream for hundreds of miles, and waterfalls and rapids may block the way. But these fish are good jumpers. They can leap eight or ten feet.

Photo courtesy of Fisheries and Oceans, Government of Canada

Photo courtesy of Fisheries and Oceans, Government of Canada

Many are caught. Human fishermen like to catch them. So do animals.
The Alaska brown bear is the best fisherman of all.

These fish are . . .

Photo courtesy of Fisheries and Oceans, Government of Canada

salmon. These two Pacific salmon have reached their goal. The mother has turned on her side and is digging a nest with her tail. The father stands guard. When salmon go home to spawn, their bodies change. Their color darkens, and their skin becomes spongy. Look at the father's jaws. The lower one is now hooked at the end. The upper one has grown longer. The front teeth are bigger. No one knows why these changes take place.

By egg-laying time, salmon are tired and bruised. They have not eaten during their long swim. They have used up their body fat. Once they have spawned, Pacific salmon die. Some Atlantic salmon also die, but some return to the sea.

The mother lives in warm seas and feeds on plants. She has no teeth, but her jaws have sharp edges that she uses to tear off bits of plants. When it is time for her to lay her eggs, she comes ashore. Here are her tracks.

Florida News Bureau

The mother pulls herself over the sand with her flippers. It's hard work because she weighs about three hundred pounds. From time to time, she stops and sighs. Then she moves on.

Far up the beach the mother makes her nest in a place the sea cannot reach. She makes a hollow in the sand. In the hollow she makes a round, deep hole. She digs with one hind flipper, then the other. This hole is the nest. In it she lays her eggs.

The mother lays about one hundred big white eggs. Nothing stops her once she starts to lay. You can walk up and touch her or even use flashbulbs to take photographs of her. She goes right on laying.

When she has finished laying her eggs, the mother fills the hole with sand. Then she flops around on top of it. Now the nest is hidden, and the mother pulls herself away to the sea. Her job is done.

The eggs stay in the warm damp sand. If no animal finds and eats them, they hatch out in two to three months.

The babies dig their way out of the nest and hurry toward the sea. Danger is all around them. Many land animals like to catch and eat them on their way to the sea. The sea is safer, but even so, many will be eaten by crabs and fish.

The babies have many relatives. Some live on land. Some live in fresh water. Some live in warm seas. Most of the relatives have legs.

These animals are . . .

41

turtles that live in the sea. This one is called a green turtle.

A baby green turtle is so small you could hold it in your hand. If it is not eaten, it will grow up into a very large turtle like this one.

Photo Trends
Ross E. Hutchins

The mother lays her eggs on just one kind of plant. Its leaves are the only ones her young will eat. She lays two or three eggs on each plant. In this way, all the young will have plenty of food. They are big eaters.

The eggs are tiny and pale green. The mother does not need to take care of them.

A few days later, the eggs begin to hatch. A tiny animal crawls out of each egg. It is as thin as a hair, and it is born hungry. First it eats the eggshell. Then it starts on the leaf. It looks something like a worm, but it is really a . . .

caterpillar. The mother was not a caterpillar. She had six legs and brightly colored wings.

This young caterpillar eats and eats. It eats one milkweed leaf after another. It grows bigger and bigger. From time to time it sheds its skin. Its skin does not grow along with its body, as yours does. Instead, it splits along the back, and the caterpillar steps out of it, wearing a baggy new skin.

This caterpillar is about two weeks old. It has black and yellow stripes. It is two inches long, and it weighs 2,500 times more than it did at birth. Soon it will change from a caterpillar into something else.

The caterpillar stops eating and crawls away. It needs a certain kind of place to stay while changing its form. The place can be the underside of a leaf or fence. It can be a twig or a stalk. On it the caterpillar spins a small silk pad. It hangs head down from the pad. Its body curls into a J-shape.

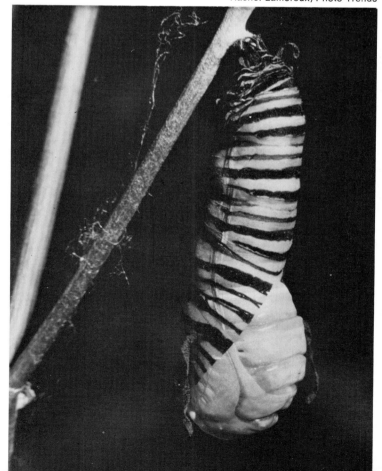

The caterpillar sheds its skin for the last time. Beneath the skin is a soft shell. It is green with touches of gold. Soon the shell hardens.

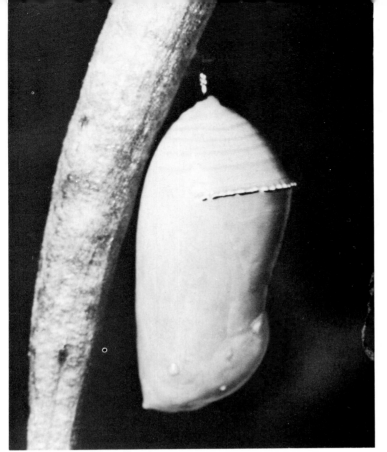

Rachel Lamoreux/Photo Trends

Shaw/Annan

For two weeks the shell simply hangs there. It doesn't move, but inside, great changes are taking place.

One day the shell splits open. An insect slowly works its way out. What is it? At first it looks like a piece of crumpled wet paper.

46

The young animal rests. Its body hardens. Its orange-and-black wings spread out and dry. This young animal will spend its days flying about and feeding. But it will no longer eat leaves.

It is a . . .

butterfly, a monarch butterfly. It feeds from flowers. A butterfly has two feelers with knobs at the ends. These serve as its nose. They guide it to sweet-smelling flowers. To feed, the butterfly uncoils a long tube and sucks the flower's nectar.

In autumn, great clouds of young monarchs fly south for the winter. Some travel a thousand miles or more. In spring they start north, laying eggs as they go.

Butterflies have short lives. The monarchs that start north never arrive, but their young continue the journey.

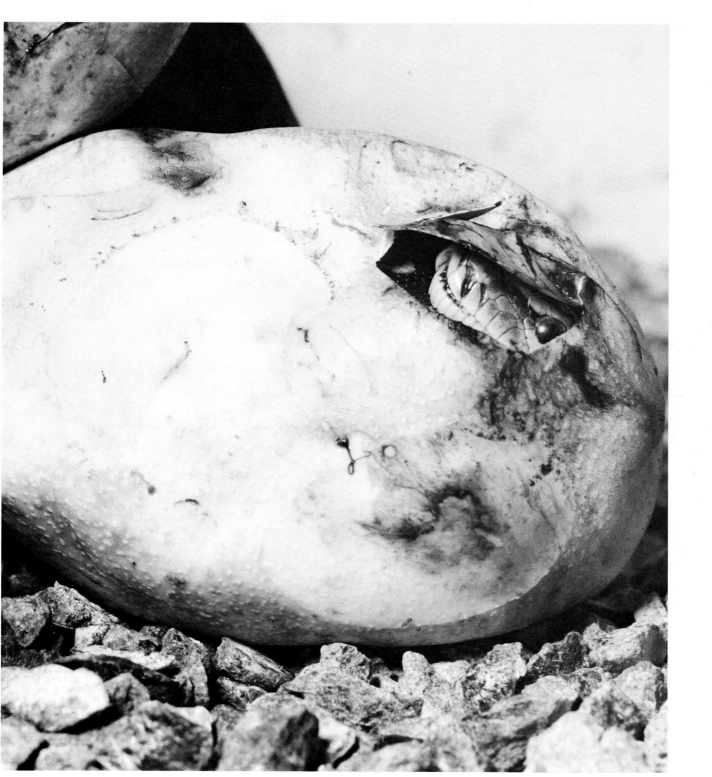

This is not a potato. It is an egg, with a tough, leathery shell. The baby animal inside has just used its egg tooth to cut a slit in the shell. Now it is resting and taking its first look at the world.

New York Zoological Society photo

T. S. Satyan/Photo Trends

The baby is in no hurry to leave the shell. It may stay there for hours. It may stay a few days. From time to time it sticks its head out. Then it pulls back into the shell.

Soon the baby will be out of the shell and ready to hunt. It may hunt on the ground or from a tree. It's a good climber and can hang by its tail, waiting for prey. This baby animal is big and strong. Right now it's two and a half feet long.

How can it still fit in its shell? That's easy, if you've guessed what kind of animal this is.

It's a baby snake, and it's coiled inside the shell. In this photograph part of the shell has been cut away to show what's inside.

Now the baby is out and away. Look sharp, and you can see its tongue. Like all snakes, it keeps flicking its tongue in and out. It uses its tongue for both tasting and smelling.

What kind of snake is it? Here are some clues.

The snake lives wild in India. Many zoos have this kind of snake—it's one of the biggest in the world. It grows eighteen to twenty feet long. When hunting, it strikes with its sharp teeth. Its body coils around the prey and squeezes. When the prey can no longer breathe, it dies. The snake swallows it whole, head first. All snakes can open their mouths very wide. When full-grown, this one can swallow a whole pig or a goat. It can swallow an antelope, horns and all.

It is a . . .

python. It is an Indian rock python. The mother python in the photograph above is laying eggs. She may lay from fifty to one hundred. The eggs take about two months to hatch. During that time, the mother stays coiled around them. She does not even eat.

Most egg-laying snakes do not guard their eggs. They find a safe place, lay their eggs, and go away. The Indian rock python stays with her eggs and leaves only when the young start to hatch. They can take care of themselves.

Some snakes do not lay their eggs. Instead, the eggs stay in the mother's body. These eggs do not have shells. In place of a shell, each has a thin sac. The young snake develops inside this sac. When the young are born, they quickly break out of their sacs. They, too, are ready to take care of themselves.

This is the mother's bill. It looks like the bill of a duck, but it isn't. This mother is not a bird—or a snake, or a fish, or an insect.

The bill is soft and leathery. The two holes are for breathing. The bill is full of nerves. The mother uses it to feel for food underwater.

This is one of her feet. It is broad and webbed and useful for swimming. The foot also has strong claws, which the mother uses for digging. Most of the time she lives with her mate in a burrow dug in a riverbank. At egg-laying time, the mother digs a second burrow and makes a nest in it.

The mother gathers leaves, grass, and reeds. Curving her tail around them, she carries them into the burrow and uses them to line the nest. She lays two small rubbery eggs in her nest. They are about the size of sparrow eggs.

For ten to fourteen days the mother curls around the eggs to keep them warm. When the young hatch, they are tiny—about half an inch long. They cannot see. They have no fur. At first there is nothing to eat. Then the mother's milk starts. It breaks out like sweat, on her underside, and the young lap it up.

The nursing mother is hungry. She leaves her young in the burrow and goes hunting. She slides into the water and dives. She looks something like a beaver, but she isn't one. Beavers don't lay eggs.

She gathers worms, shrimps, tadpoles, and other small creatures. She stores them in her cheek pouches. She comes to the surface to eat.

The babies leave the burrow when they are four months old. By then they can see. They have fur. They are ready to swim and hunt. Have you guessed what animal this is? Here are a few more clues.

This animal is rare. It is hard to raise in zoos because it is shy. If you want to see one, you may have to go to Australia. That's where it lives.

This animal is a . . .

platypus. The platypus is a mammal, an animal that nurses its young on milk. In all the world only two kinds of mammals lay eggs. The platypus is one. The other is the spiny anteater, which also lives in Australia.

Eggs and More Eggs

Here is the egg you know best. A hen laid it. What's inside the shell? There's the yolk and the white, but that's not all.

The next time you open an egg, let it slide into a saucer. Wait a minute or two. Then look carefully at the yolk. Near the top you'll see a tiny white spot. It is the part that can grow into a chick. The yolk and white are food for the chick. The shell is its house.

A hen can lay eggs by herself. But she cannot make chicks by herself. Something else is needed to make the white spot grow. That something is a seed, or sperm, from a rooster.

When a hen and rooster mate, the rooster's sperm goes into the hen's body. The sperm are tiny, with long tails. They swim up a tube in the hen's body. They join the eggs, which are mostly yolk.

One sperm joins with one egg. The egg moves down the tube. Along the way, white is added to the yolk. The shell is added last.

The hen lays her eggs. She keeps them warm. About twenty-one days later, the chicks hatch out. Sometimes an egg has a double yolk. Then two chicks hatch out.

Jerome Wexler/Photo Researchers, Inc.

Frogs mate in another way. A male frog rides on the female's back. She sheds eggs in the water, and he sheds sperm. One sperm joins one egg. A new frog life begins.

A mother salmon sheds her eggs in her nest. The father sheds sperm in the nest. When a sperm joins an egg, a new salmon life begins.

That's the way much new life begins—a sperm joins an egg. It happens with almost any kind of animal you could name.

Did you know that elephants grow from eggs? They do. So do whales, dogs, cats, horses, mice, bats. You, too, grew from an egg. But these are not the kind of eggs you find in nests.

These eggs are tiny. They have almost no food in them. They don't need it. They have no shells. They don't need shells. These eggs stay inside the mother's body. That's where they grow into baby animals. The mother's body makes food for her babies. It acts as their shell, or house.

These babies don't hatch out. They are born live.

Only two kinds of mammals lay eggs. All other kinds give birth to their young. Some kinds of young are helpless. Some can walk or swim. But all need help. No baby mammal can take care of itself. Mother mammals take care of their young. Some father mammals help.

Eggs come in many sizes and colors. Yet they are all alike in one way. When a sperm joins an egg, a new life begins. It may turn out to be a frog, a chick, an elephant, or something else. But it is always the same kind as its parents.

Index

DATE DUE

Brodart Co.   Cat. # 55 137 001   Printed in USA